The Slave Trade

John D. Clare

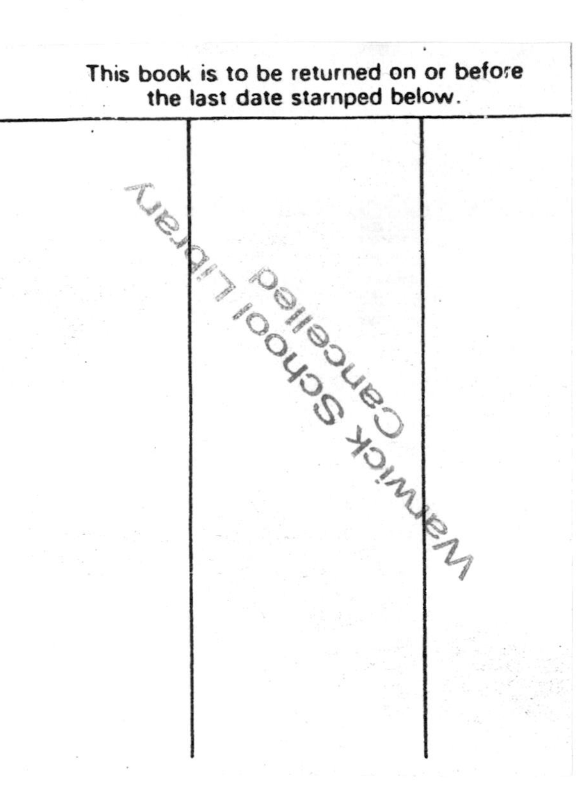

The Publishers would like to thank the following for permission to reproduce copyright material:
Photo credits p.5 © Wilberforce House, Hull City Museums and Art Galleries, UK/The Bridgeman Art Library; pp.6–7 These are artworks based on the TV series; **pp.6–7** artworks; **pp.8 & 10** © National Maritime Museum, Greenwich, London; **p.11** Bibliotheque de L'Arsenal, Paris, France/Archives Charmet/The Bridgeman Art Library; **p.13** Yale Center for British Art, Paul Mellon Collection, USA/The Bridgeman Art Library; **p.14** Royal Albert Memorial Museum, Exeter, Devon, UK/The Bridgeman Art Library; **p.15** *tr & b* Mary Evans Picture Library, *tl* © Christie's Images/Corbis; **p.16** *t* akg-images, *b* Bibliotheque des Arts Decoratifs, Paris, France/Archives Charmet/The Bridgeman Art Library; **p.17** The Art Archive/Geographical Society Paris/Dagli Orti; **p.18** Private Collection/© Michael Graham-Stewart/The Bridgeman Art Library; **p.19** Mary Evans ILN Pictures; **p.20** © Bettmann/Corbis; **p.21** © Bristol City Museum and Art Gallery, UK/The Bridgeman Art Library; **p.23** *t & c* © Visual Arts Library (London)/Alamy, *b* © The Print Collector/Alamy; **p.24** © Corbis; **p.25** © Mary Evans Picture Library/Alamy; **p.26** © Corbis; **p.27** akg-images; **p.29** Musee des Beaux-Arts, Chartres, France/The Bridgeman Art Library; **p.30** © Bettmann/Corbis; **p.31** American Antiquarian Society, Worcester, Massachusetts, USA/The Bridgeman Art Library; **p.34** *tl* © Courtesy of the Warden and Scholars of New College, Oxford/The Bridgeman Art Library, *tr* © Mary Evans Picture Library/Alamy, *cl* Hulton Archive/Getty Images, *cr* © National Portrait Gallery, London, *b* Parliamentary Archives, London, HL/PO/JO/10/8/106; **p.35** *tl* Osterley Park, Middlesex, UK/The Stapleton Collection/The Bridgeman Art Library, *tr* Mary Evans Picture Library, *cl* © Classic Image/Alamy, *c* © Chicago History Museum, USA/The Bridgeman Art Library, *cr* American Philosophical Society, *b* © Visual Arts Library (London)/Alamy; **p.36** Walden Media/Bristol Bay/Ingenious Film Partners/Roadside Attractions/Courtesy of the Ronald Grant Archive; **p.37** *t* © National Portrait Gallery, London, *b* Stamp Designs © Royal Mail Group Ltd, Reproduced by kind permission of Royal Mail Group Ltd. All Rights Reserved; **p.38** *tl* © Wilberforce House, Hull City Museums and Art Galleries, UK/The Bridgeman Art Library, *r* Royal Albert Memorial Museum, Exeter, Devon, UK/The Bridgeman Art Library, *bl* © Visual Arts Library (London)/Alamy, *br* © Bristol City Museum and Art Gallery, UK/The Bridgeman Art Library; **p.39** *tr* National Portrait Gallery, *tl* British Library/HIP/TopFoto, *bl* Private Collection/The Bridgeman Art Library, *br* © Visual Arts Library (London)/Alamy; **p.40** © The Print Collector/Alamy; **p.41** Private Collection/The Stapleton Collection/The Bridgeman Art Library; **pp.42 & 43** akg-images; **p.44** Ascott, The Anthony de Rothschild Collection (The National Trust), © NTPL/John Hammond; **p.47** © Wilberforce House, Hull City Museums and Art Galleries, UK/The Bridgeman Art Library; **p.48** Andrew Dunsmore/Rex Features.

Orders: please contact Bookpoint Ltd, 130 Milton Park, Abingdon, Oxon OX14 4SB. Telephone: (44) 01235 827720. Fax: (44) 01235 400454. Lines are open 9.00–5.00, Monday to Saturday, with a 24-hour message answering service. Visit our website at www.hoddereducation.co.uk

First published in 2008 by
Hodder Education,
Part of Hachette Livre UK
338 Euston Road
London NW1 3BH

Impression number 5 4 3 2 1
Year 2012 2011 2010 2009 2008

Cover photo shows a Wedgwood medallion, courtesy of the American Philosophical Society
Illustrations by Tony Randell, Richard Duszczak and Tony Jones
Typeset in Imperial 11/13.5pt by Lorraine Inglis Design
Printed in Italy

A catalogue record for this title is available from the British Library

ISBN: 978 0340 957 707

Contents

Starter: Setting the question

First thoughts: Should we apologise?

To be clear from the start: slavery – and the slave trade – is wrong.

In 2001, the United Nations' World Conference against Racism declared:

> *'Slavery and the slave trade were appalling tragedies [and] a crime against humanity ...'*

In 2006, Britain's Prime Minister Tony Blair wrote in the Black newspaper *New Nation*:

> *'how profoundly shameful the slave trade was [and] to express our deep sorrow that it ever happened.'*

The big question

Some people thought Mr Blair was wrong to say this. Why should the British people, they said, apologise for something that their ancestors did hundreds of years ago – especially when it was not only legal at the time, but was considered normal and right, even by the Africans themselves?

For other people, expressing 'deep sorrow' did not go far enough. Many African countries at the 2001 conference demanded that Britain should be made to pay compensation – 'reparations' – to repair the damage done.

SOURCE 1

Are the Italians planning reparations for the misdeeds of the Roman Empire? Will the French apologise for invading us in 1066? History is history, it cannot be expected that people should apologise ... for the actions of their forebears.

A comment on the BBC *'Have Your Say'* debate about reparations (March 2007).

SOURCE 2

An apology is just the start – words mean nothing. We're talking about ... financial compensation. If we do not deal with this now it is tantamount to saying that you can commit crimes against humanity, against African people, and get away with it.

Esther Stanford, of the Pan-African Reparation Coalition, taking part in the BBC debate.

Activities

1. **Think of situations where you might apologise for doing something, even though you did not realise you were doing wrong at the time.**
2. **Suggest a caption for Source 3, on page 5.**
3. **Would you choose to side with Source 1 or Source 2? Write down your 'First thoughts on the slave trade'. Was Tony Blair right to apologise?**

SOURCE 3

***Slave Traders on the Coast of Africa*, a painting by A.F. Biard (1833).**

1 The triangular trade

Interpretations: The slave trade – TV-style

In 1976 the author Alex Haley published his book *Roots*, tracing his family back to Kunta Kinte, a 15-year-old boy living in Africa. The book became a huge success – 130 million people watched the TV mini-series based on the book. *Roots* fictionalised Kunta Kinte's story, fleshing out the facts with ideas that Haley had about the slave trade.

Critics say that its depiction of life in Africa is too Americanised, and that the story is almost wholly made up, but *Roots* created our modern idea of what the slave trade was like.

Kunta Kinte lives in Africa with his loving family. At 15, he becomes a man; to do this he has to learn how to wrestle, and he is circumcised. The scenes are happy and his life is idyllic. He meets a pretty girl called Fanta, from another tribe.

One day, when he is looking in the forest for some wood for a drum, Kunta is captured by slave-traders. He is marched to the coast, and imprisoned in a wooden cage. With horror, he finds that Fanta and Wrestler (the great warrior who taught him to wrestle) have been captured too.

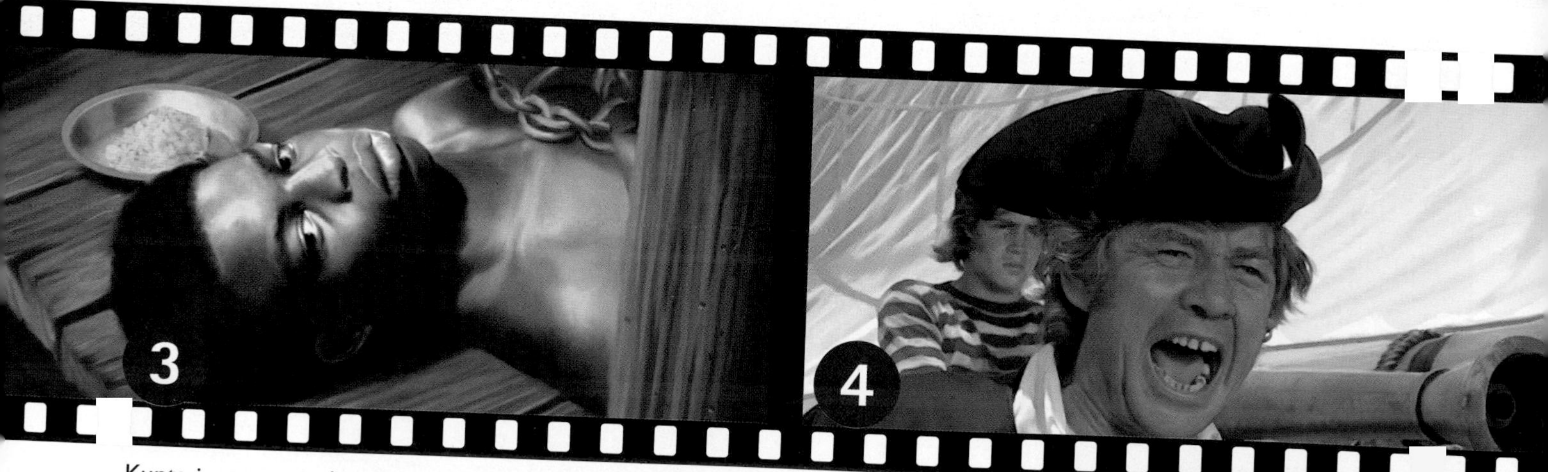

Kunta is put on a slave ship and transported to America. The captain – Captain Davies – hates the slave trade, but is powerless to help the slaves, and he ends up accepting a female slave as a 'belly-warmer' in his bed.

Slater, the Third Mate, is a brutal and callous racist, who whips and tortures the slaves, keeps them below deck in terrible conditions, and delights in giving the men 'their ease' with the female slaves – including Fanta. Kunta himself almost goes mad, but then realises that he can stay free in his mind.

The slaves are brought on board and forced to exercise (by dancing to music). Some slaves jump overboard and drown, rather than face the voyage. Wrestler and Kunta lead a mutiny, but it is put down by gunfire, and Wrestler is killed.

When the ship docks in America, the company agent (Mr Carrington) praises the 'golden triangle' by which British ships take slaves to America. But the ship smells so bad that he has to hold a handkerchief over his nose.

The slaves are prepared for sale. Their sores are daubed with tar, and their bodies oiled to make them look healthy. Kunta is examined like a beast, and auctioned to a planter called Mr Reynolds.

Kunta is given a new name: 'Toby'. Mr Reynolds hands him over to Mr Ames, the plantation overseer, who whips him into submission.

Toby keeps trying to run away, but when he eventually finds Fanta, she does not want to know him. She is Maggie now, she tells him, and she has forgotten 'that African talk'. Toby is captured, and his foot is chopped off to stop him doing it again.

Activities

1. **Study the story of *Roots*. Remember that it is just a fictional story. Make a list of the nine main events of the story.**
2. **Imagine you are Kunta Kinte. Tell the story from your 'own' point of view.**
3. **Now tell the story from the point of view of the following people:**
   a) Captain Davies
   b) Mr Reynolds
   c) Mr Carrington
   d) Slater.

Knowledge: The triangular trade

In *Roots*, Carrington – the agent who met Kunta Kinte's ship when it docked in America – made the slave trade sound very simple, and very easy:

> ‘*Thus does heaven smile on us, point to point in a golden triangle: tobacco – trade goods – slaves – tobacco – trade goods and so on* ad infinitum. *All profit, sir, and none the loser for it.*’

Script of the TV series *Roots* (1977).

The golden triangle

The basic idea was very simple.

A ship was loaded up in ENGLAND with a cargo of stuff which was much in demand in Africa – cloth and hats; iron bars and saucepans; guns, gunpowder and shot; salt; and trinkets such as beads and bells.

The captain then sailed to AFRICA. There, he bartered his cargo for slaves. Some captains preferred to do this direct with the **African rulers**, but by the end of the eighteenth century most captains simply stopped at one of the many ‘factories’ which had been set up along the coast. In 1700 a slave could be bought for as little as £3. By 1800 the price was more like £25 each.

This picture shows the factory on Factory Island on the Isles de Los, West Africa. The factories offered an ‘all-in’ service to the slave-trading captain: negotiating slaves from the African rulers; providing lodgings, a pilot and interpreter; supplying rice and grain for the next voyage; and even mending the boat in their shipyards if necessary. By 1800, all a captain had to do was hand over his cargo and wait.

In *Roots*, Slater, the evil Third Mate, talks about a ‘tight pack’ or a ‘loose pack’ of slaves – meaning how many slaves he could get into the hold – but after 1788 a Law of Parliament laid down how many slaves a British captain could take on board – five slaves for every 3 tons of tonnage.

So, now loaded with slaves, the **slave-traders** set off on the month-or-so-long voyage to THE AMERICAS (the so-called ‘Middle Passage’). The captain would try to arrive in January, during the sugar-cane harvest, when the demand from the **planters** for slaves, and the prices, were highest. The average price of a slave in the West Indies was £20 in 1700, rising to about £35 in 1800. There the captain handed over the slaves to his employer's agents, who sold the slaves at auction.

According to the textbooks, a captain would then buy a cargo of those goods much in demand in Britain – sugar, rum, cotton and tobacco. He would sail home and sell those, also at a profit.

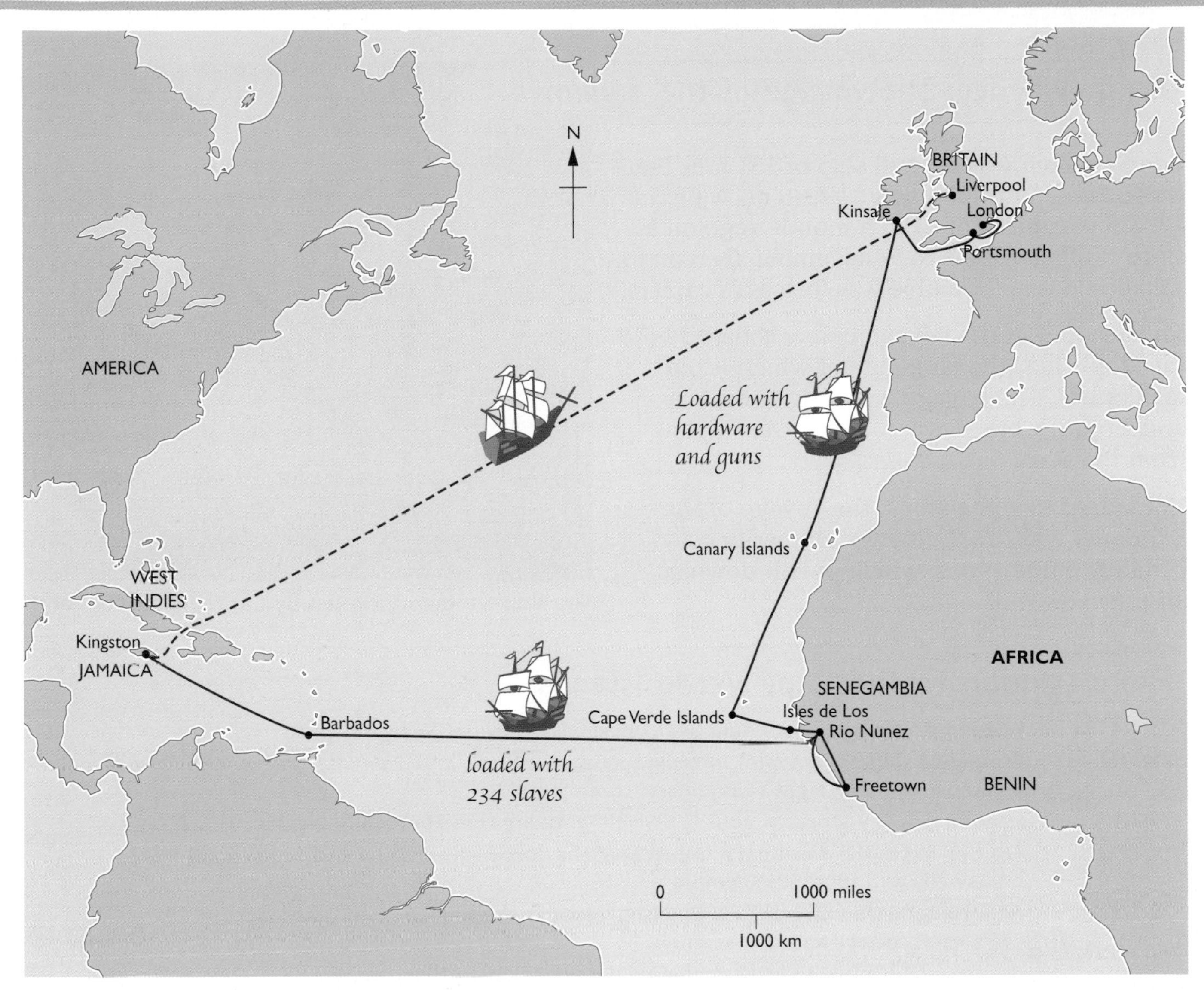

The triangular trade, showing the voyage of the *Sandown*, 1793–94.

That, of course, is just the theory. The truth was much more complicated:

- Many British voyages were chartered for two legs only – from Britain to Africa and from Africa to the West Indies – where the captain and crew were sacked and left to make their own way back home. The owners then re-hired the ship to West Indian merchants who used it solely to take their goods to Britain.
- There was no 'triangular trade' for slave-traders from America and Brazil, who simply sailed to Africa, picked up slaves, and sailed back home.
- Slave ships met all kinds of difficulties, including pirates and enemy navies, slave uprisings, mutiny and shipwreck.

Activities

1. Use the information on page 8 to make three lists:
   a) the three places in the triangle (in capitals)
   b) the three kinds of people who took part in the trade (in red type)
   c) what the three kinds of people had to offer and what they wanted.
2. Using the figures for the prices of slaves in Africa and America in 1700 and 1800, work out how much profit a slave-trader could make per slave in 1700, and in 1800.

Using evidence: The voyage of the *Sandown*

The *Sandown* was a small ship of 151 tons that was 82 ft (25 m) long and 21 ft (6 m) wide. In 1793 it was hired at £125 a month to go on a slave-trading voyage to Senegambia, then on to Jamaica. Samuel Gamble was the ship's captain.

The account of the voyage below is based on the ship's log (the language of which is old-fashioned). The voyage was risky – France and Britain were at war – and it went wrong from the start.

Compared to some ships, the voyage of the *Sandown* was not a disaster. But it almost certainly made a loss, which puts it down as an unsuccessful voyage.

The ship *Sandown*, drawn by Captain Samuel Gamble.

From London to the Cape Verde Islands

23/1/1793	Loaded provisions – including beef, pork, tripe, powder kegs and shot.
28/1/93	'Employ'd shipping people', including a Second Mate, a boatswain, a carpenter, a cooper, a cook, a steward, eight seamen and three 'boys'.
29/1/93	Loaded 'Sundry stores, 4 guns, 2 Swivell guns, big Iron Handcuffs, Neck chains & collars.'
19/2/93	On this night, the royal navy 'impressed' [i.e. forcibly recruited and took away] his boatswain, and six of his seamen.
23/2/93	At midnight, the navy arrived and impressed more men, including the Second Mate, carpenter, cooper and two seamen.
1/4/93	Recruited 13 more seamen, including 'James Atkins, a Black cook'.
7/4/93	'Fresh breezes with hazy weather ... at 7 hoisted the pinnacle at 10 got underweigh'. Sailed to Portsmouth, looking to join a convoy guarded by royal navy vessels (to protect him against French warships).
27/4/93	Met a packet ship which warned him of pirates nearby.
28/4/93	Docked in Kinsale in Ireland – thought it poor and dirty.
2/5/93	Took on five more seamen. Dismissed one man (who didn't like the sea) and a second who had an infectious disease ('not able to do his duty').
4/5/93	Set sail again. 82 ships in the convoy.
9/5/93	Waited for the slower ships to catch up. Gamble complained that he was losing 40 or 50 miles a day.
19/5/93	Docked in the Canary Islands.
20/5/93	Set sail again, 'carrying all sail to best advantage. Ships company all well and employ'd painting etc. Carpenter and Cooper at sundry jobs.'
21/5/93	Uneventful voyage and good weather: 'this certainly is a glorious Climate'.
23/5/93	'At 2p.m. the Ships Company went through the old Custom of Shaving, and Ducking, all that never cross'd the Tropic of Cancer before.'
27/5/93	Docked in the Cape Verde Islands – visited the Governor.
2/6/93	Set sail again.
4/6/93	'Great part of the Ships Company very much afflicted with blind Biles [fever], two in the Doctors list [i.e. too ill to work].'

In Africa

11/6/93 Expected to find the Iles de Los but couldn't because the navigation charts were wrong.

12/6/93 Docked at Factory Island.

[Gamble could have refitted and bought slaves here but, 'everything here being in such a state of confusion' because of the war, he chose another factory.]

'Made a Barter with Mr James Walker for 250 Slaves for the whole of my cargo which amounts to £5,721.'

2/7/93 Sailed up the Rio Nunez to Walker's factory. 'Dreadful Thunder, lightning, and rain, attended at times with a heavy Turnado … This Country appears to be at variance with Mankind … Wild Bees and Large flies very troublesome in the day, with Muskeros in the Night … so that a European richly deserves what he gains here.'

18/7/93 Yellow fever struck – sixteen sailors 'down in a raging fever … Made application to Mr Walker for to find a place fit for a Hospital, got fires in the house and sent on shore all the Sick that were fit to remove.'

1/8/93 '17 in the Doctors list out of 21 of our Number … Those that are not delirious, are peevish and Childish as if in their first state of Infancy.'

6/8/93 'I am afraid the Decks being leakey that some of the Cargo will be damag'd and no person on board able to assist me in examining.'

7/8/93 'Departed this life Charles McLean, Aged 25 Years.'

9/8/93 'All hands sick but me and the Doctor and he complains very much.'

22/8/93 'I find my self very Feverish Squamish and sick today this being the third attack since I came into the river.'

12/9/93 'Ships Crew no fevers amongst them, have learn'd such an Idle, Indolent, habit: that it's nearly impossible to make them keep themselves clean.'

15/9/93 'Ships company begin to be bad with the flux [diarrhoea], those that are not affected are so Lazey the Doctor cannot persuade them to walk about.'

20/9/93 'Mr Horrocks dead, being sick only two days.'

11/10/93 'Cooper so weak & Sickly that he cannot trim the Water Casks. Rest of the Ships Crew little better than dead.'

25/10/93 Walker began delivering slaves, a few at a time.

11/12/93 'Departed this life James Ronald, Cooper, Aged 23 Years.'

12/12/93 40 slaves on board. Bought some rice.

18/12/93 'Fevers and Ague rage very much. Begin to be very uneasy, there being no prospect of soon getting away and all Hands very sickly. The Medicines nearly finished.'

20/12/93 'Departed this life after a Lingering illness of 5 Months Dennis Mcarty, Seaman, Aged 36 Years.'

28/12/93 (–15 Feb 1794) Gamble went to Sierra Leone to collect 57 slaves. When he returned he found another seaman had died and there had been a slave mutiny – 'seven Men & one Woman drowned. One Man-Boy and a Man run away'. By this time, 134 slaves had been delivered.

A coffle (travelling line) of slaves in Senegal, *c.* 1780, drawn from life.

On the Middle Passage

8/3/94	Walker finished delivering all 250 slaves, although deaths and the mutiny had reduced the number to 234.
19/3/94	Ready to depart – waiting only for Mr Walker to provide a pilot. Took on nine new sailors. Worried by news of French attacks.
27/3/94	Set sail.
28/3/94	'Slaves very Sea Sick, cannot eat their Food.'
3/4/94	'At 5p.m. the Doctor Amputated a Mans finger that was begun to Mortify, having been bit by another Slave. At 6p.m. he departed this Life.'
6/4/94	'Found a Man Slave stow'd away in the Hold, got him up and secur'd him likewise several others that were found could get their Hands out of Irons.'
7/4/94	'Slaves afflicted with Billious Complaints likewise with the Worms.'
10/4/94	'Employ'd cleaning ship Shaving Slaves & filling up salt water. Several of both Whites and Blacks in the Doctors list.'
15/4/94	'Slaves complain that it is very Cold. A number of the Women very Meagure. Men in good Spirits. 9 in the Doctors list.' Found that some of the water casks were leaking.
16/4/94	'Buried one Woman & 1 Girl Slaves.'
17/4/94	'Buried a Man Boy Slave. Several others very poorly.'
20/4/94	'At 10AM counted the Slaves Viz 86 Men, 29 Mboys, 30 Boys, 40 Women, 13 Wgirls & 28 Girls. Total on Board 226 – 10 lost in the Mutiny & 14 Dead.'
21/4/94	Buried a boy.
22/4/94	'Departed this Life John Cameron chief mate Aged 27 Years of the Dropsy, not having had Six Weeks good Health since we left London.'
24/4/94	'Buried a Man Slave. Ships Company rather Sickly 5 in the D list. Several Slaves poorly, the rest in good Spirits Owing to the Sun be hot.'
25/4/94	'Slaves very Sickly Buried 1 Boy and 1 Girl Slaves. Ships Company Sickly 5 in the Doctors list. Disorders amongst both Whites and Blacks. Flux and Scurvy with Slight Fevers. Came to a resolution of calling at Barbadoes to fill up our Water and get some Vegetables &c to refresh the Slaves and Crew.'
26/4/94	'Ships Company Sickly. Buried two Men Slaves.'
29/4/94	Docked in the Barbadoes. 'Sundry people left the Ship without leave.'
30/4/94	In all 17 crew ran away. 'Buried two Women Girl Slaves.'
1/5/94	'Buried a Woman Girl and a Boy. 8 in the Doctors List.' Gamble asked for permission to sell a couple of Slaves to raise some money (but was not allowed).
2/5/94	'Went on board HMS Vanguard to beg Capt Stanhope to take me under his protection. He not being on board, I was told that the Ship would be confiscated tomorrow. & they would unship her rudder and carry her Sails on shore.'
3/5/94	The voyage was in danger of going bankrupt. 'Finding Money so scarce and none to be had on any Security Mr Bartin beg'd that I would make my way to Jamaica. At 1AM got underway. Our Ship in great Distress, only Myself, Mr Apsey, Mr Griffith, Doctor, Alex Chisholm & Geo Drummond to look after Ship & Slaves.'
6/5/94	'Cannot carry sails for want of hands to take in sail. Slaves rather sickly. Buried Woman Slave.'
7/5/94	'Slaves very Sickly. Buried 1 Man & 1 Woman slave.'
8/5/94	'Slaves complain very much of the Gripes and Looseness.'
10/5/94	'Slaves still complain very much of the Gripes. 7 in Doctors list, tried everything on board boat, fear nothing gives them relief.'

In Jamaica

An engraving of Kingston and Port Royal in Jamaica.

12/5/94	Berthed at Kingston, Jamaica. Found Yellow Fever raging and nobody buying slaves. 'Am informed that there's upwards of 3,000 Slaves in Harbour for Sale and in this last twelve months there has been 60,000 Sold. 9 Slaves sickly on board.'
14/5/94	'Receiv'd on board fresh Beef and some Vegetables. Buried a Girl.'
17/5/94	'5 Sick Slaves sent on shore. Several complaining. Employ'd looking after them. Receiv'd meat for them.'
19/5/94	'Several Spaniards came on board to look at the Cargo. Delivr'd One Woman Slave as ordered. Buried a Woman Slave.'
21/5/94	'Am very ill of the Gout and Rheumatism myself & cannot go about any duty.'
22/5/94	'Was ordered by Angus Kennedy to go down on shore to sick lodgings, having declared that if I did not go he would make me.'
24/5/94	'Went on board the Ship to look after, and see that the Slaves were attended.'
26/5/94	'Slaves go off very slow (Market glutted).'
27/5/94	'Deliver'd up the Ships papers, and a Copy of the Ship Disbursements &c. to Messrs Kennedy Charterers of the Said Ship *Sandown*.'
15/6/94	'The Sale of Negroes here very indifferent at present.' All but four of the slaves were sold by the middle of July.

And home

Gamble was ill into July, after which he 'got better fast and continued to do so'. When he was well enough, he got a passage home on the ship *Benson* bound for Liverpool, arriving home on 11/10/94.

Activities

1. Read pages 10–13. List all the problems that Captain Gamble faced on his journey.
2. Use the entries from 20/4/94 to 15/6/94 to work out how many slaves Gamble finally sold.
   a) Guessing £35 per slave, calculate his total income from the voyage.
   b) Work out the percentage death rate for slaves.
3. Use pages 11–12 to find out how many of the 21 crew died. Work out the percentage death rate.
4. From the total income, deduct the cost of the cargo (see 12/6/93), the cost of the ship (£125 a month), as well as £231 for other costs, to calculate his final profit for the voyage.

CHAPTER 2 The slaves' story

Using evidence: At home in Africa

The TV series *Roots* showed Africa as an idyllic, happy society, based on the family and the tribe.

How true is this picture of life in Africa in the eighteenth century? In 1789, a former slave called Olaudah Equiano wrote his autobiography. Here he describes life in Benin:

SOURCE 1

I was born in Benin, in the year 1745, in a charming fruitful valley … My father was one of the elders or chiefs, and was styled 'Embrence'; a term, as I remember, of the highest honour …

We are a nation of dancers, musicians and poets … As our lifestyle is simple, our luxuries are few.

Before we taste food we always wash our hands: indeed our cleanliness at all times is extreme … We have no strong or alcoholic drink; our main drink is palm wine … Our houses are always built of stakes driven into the ground, crossed with wattles, neatly plastered and thatched with reeds … The whole neighbourhood help in building them and in return get, and expect, no other reward than a feast.

Portrait of Equiano.

Our wants are few and easily supplied … Our land is uncommonly rich and fruitful, and produces all kinds of vegetables in great abundance … Farming is our chief employment; and everyone, even the children and women, are engaged in it.

Everyone contributes something to the common welfare; and as we do not know idleness, we have no beggars … Those benefits are felt by us in the general healthiness of the people … Our women were in my eyes at least uncommonly graceful, alert and modest … They are also remarkably cheerful.

Olaudah Equiano, *An Interesting Narrative* (1789).

Equiano was a Black African and former slave living in England, who wrote his book as part of the campaign to abolish the slave trade. There is evidence that he was not born in Africa, but in Carolina in America.

Activities

1. **Make a list of all the good things Equiano tells us about Africa. What is the message he was trying to get across about Africans?**
2. **Study Source 1 at word level. Is there anything which makes you believe that Equiano was genuinely remembering his life in Africa?**
3. **Is there anything which makes you suspect that he was not writing about genuine memories?**
4. **Choose the image from Sources 2–4 which would best show: 'What life in Africa was like in the 18th century'. Think about what the picture shows, but also how true-to-life it is likely to be.**

SOURCE 2

Eugène Frometin visited Africa twice, and made such detailed notes and sketches that his paintings are regarded as historical records as well as works of art. This painting is of *The Oasis at Lagrount*, in Algeria (*c.* 1860).

SOURCE 3

This picture of an African wedding is from a book on *Religious Ceremonies and Costumes*, drawn by the French engraver Bernard Picart in 1723. Picart never left Europe, but based his drawings on descriptions by people who had been there. Picart – unlike many people at the time – tried to produce pictures that did not depict Africans as savages.

SOURCE 4

This early 20th century postcard shows an African village. A white church is in the centre of the photograph, but the comment on the postcard says that the missionaries have ruined traditional African life.

Interpretations: Africa revisited

In his book on Senegambia during the time of the slave trade, the historian Professor Boubacar Barry paints a frightening picture of West Africa.

A terrible vicious circle

This, says Barry, was the age of the *ceddo* – armed soldiers with guns. Kings kept huge armies of royal slaves, trained as warriors, who attacked neighbouring states and carried off slaves to sell to the Dutch, British and French. They had to sell slaves, says Barry, because that was the only way they could buy the guns (from the Dutch, British and French) which would stop them becoming victims of other kings trying to capture slaves to sell to the Europeans.

Fed up with this **terrible vicious circle**, and led by Muslim leaders called *marabouts*, the people of some West African states rose up and killed or drove out their *ceddo* leaders. But this did not bring the end of the slave trade. Once in power, the *marabout* leaders declared holy war against their neighbours and attacked them, enslaving all the people in the country who were not Muslims.

The reign of Lat Sukkabe Faal (1695–1720), ruler of the small state of Kajoor in Senegal, was a time of continuous warfare. He traded slaves to get himself 200 shotguns and two cannon, which he used to bring back 2,000 slaves at a time from his slaving expeditions. He ruled with terror and violence, defeated rebellions by local Muslims, and even arrested the Director-General of the French Senegal Company when he tried to stop him slave-trading with the British.

This drawing is based on a drawing by Rene de Villeneuve, who claimed he did his drawings on the spot during a two-year stay in Senegal in the 1780s. It shows a Muslim slave-trader killing the inhabitants and capturing slaves.

At the same time, a number of natural disasters swept the countryside. The years 1747–54 were years of drought and failed harvests. There were locust swarms in 1706 and 1739–41, and in 1786 the area suffered drought *and* locusts. Worst of all were the famines caused by the wars. In all, there were twelve droughts, four floods, four locust invasions, and scores of famines, mainly in 1719–25, 1729–37 and 1747–58.

During the eighteenth century the number of slaves in Senegambia grew hugely.

- Many were captured in the *ceddo* wars.
- Many non-Muslims were enslaved by their Muslim rulers.
- Many Africans voluntarily *asked* to become the slaves of wealthy men in times of famine.

By the end of the century, at least half the people of Senegambia were slaves.

A 'bottomless reservoir'

African slave-owners preferred women slaves – it was the women's job to grow corn, do the housework and have babies. European slave-traders, however, wanted men slaves to do the field work on the plantations in the Americas. It was a perfect business opportunity for wealthy Africans. They used their women slaves to have babies and grow corn. They sold their male slaves to the European slave-traders, and then they sold them the corn to keep the slaves alive on the sea journey to America.

Thus, says Professor Barry, Senegambia became:

> ‘**a bottomless reservoir** *feeding the New World with slave labour.*’

But the blame, says Barry, lay with the slave trade. It dominated the whole economy, and determined the way the Africans lived.

Samba Gelaajo Jeegi came to power in the kingdom of Futu Toro in 1725. He became a legend, armed with his shotgun 'Bubu Lowake', fighting to the sound of the war drums while the maidens sang blood-songs about the glory of death in battle.

In six years Samba fought 45 battles. He lost power in 1731, but gained it again in 1738–41, until he was murdered by one of his wives. Knowing she had poisoned his food, he still ate it in an act of bravado, saying: 'Never do I retreat before death.'

Activities

1. From pages 16–17, make a list of all the things that made life in Africa difficult.
2. Using page 16, explain in your own words how the *ceddo* states were caught in a **'terrible vicious circle'**.
3. Using page 17, explain how Senegambia became a **'bottomless reservoir'** of slaves.
4. Who do you believe – Equiano (page 14) or Barry (pages 16–17)? Why?

Using evidence: Captured!

In *Roots*, Kunta Kinte is captured as he wanders in the forest looking for wood to make a drum for his brother. How true to life was this?

Lesser pillage

In the early days of the slave trade, White slavers would land on the African coast and simply kidnap any Black Africans they could find. This was called 'lesser pillage'.

SOURCE 1

One day, when all our people were gone out to their works as usual, and only I and my dear sister were left to mind the house, two men and a woman got over our walls and in a moment seized us both, and, without giving us time to cry out, or to resist, they stopped our mouths, and ran off with us into the nearest wood. Here they tied our hands, and continued to carry us as far as they could, till night came on … the only comfort we had was bathing each other with our tears.

But alas! we were soon deprived of even the small comfort of weeping together; for my sister and I were then separated, while we lay clasped in each other's arms … while I was left in a state of distraction not to be described …

Olaudah Equiano, *An Interesting Narrative* (1789).

Equiano was a Black African and former slave living in England, who wrote his book as part of the campaign to abolish the slave trade. There is evidence that he was not captured in Africa, but was born a slave in America.

SOURCE 2

This painting, *Execrable Human Traffic*, by George Morland (1788), was the first Abolitionist protest in the visual arts. It told the story of a kind African who, having rescued some Europeans from a shipwreck, was betrayed by them and sold into slavery. The painting was given a caption from a poem: 'Lo! the poor Captive with distraction wild, Views his dear Partner torn from his embrace!'

SOURCE 3

An artist's impression of a slave raid, drawn in 1888 for the *Graphic* magazine.

SOURCE 4

On attacking a place it is the custom of the country instantly to set fire to it; and as they are all made of straw huts only, the whole is soon devoured by flames. The unfortunate inhabitants run quickly from the fire and fall into the hands of their no less merciless enemies who surround the place; the men are quickly massacred, and the women and children lashed together and made slaves.

Major Denham, *Narrative of Travels and Discoveries in Northern and Central Africa* (1826).

Denham was an English explorer who in 1822–4 made an expedition inland into western Africa.

This description of grand pillage describes an Arab slave raid. Note that – unlike British slave-traders (who wanted men who could work on the plantations in the New World) – Arab slave-traders wanted women slaves.

Grand pillage

By the end of the eighteenth century, most slave-traders worked through factors (owners of the 'factories'), who made arrangements with local rulers. The local rulers would attack neighbouring states and carry off the population of whole villages to hand over to the factors. This was called 'grand pillage'.

Activities

1. **Explain how Source 2 is similar to Source 1.**
2. **Explain how Source 3 illustrates Source 4.**
3. **Study Source 1 at word level. Can you find any evidence that Equiano may have been making up his story?**

Interpretations: Complicity

One of the things that many historians find most confusing about the slave trade is that African rulers sold their own people to the British slave-traders.

The price of a slave

The barter price of a slave in Angola was worth about £15 (in 1735) which could buy:

- **a gun and a bag of gunpowder**
- **24 bolts of different kinds of cloth**
- **10 brass pans**
- **4 pewter basins**
- **2 cases of spirits**
- **4 cutlasses**
- **2 bunches of beads**
- **3 culgees (plumes from India worn on the front of a turban)**
- **4 telescopes**
- **10 pint mugs.**

SOURCE 1

Bartering for slaves – a French engraving of c. 1830.

Activities

1. Study Source 1. Can you see evidence:
   a) that the slaves were badly treated
   b) that the slave-traders had come from Europe
   c) that the African rulers were selling slaves to them
   d) of why the Africans sold slaves to them
   e) that the slave-traders bartered for slaves
   f) of the different kinds of goods they bartered?
2. Look at the list of things which bought a slave in Angola in 1735. Work out how much these things would be worth nowadays. What does this tell you about the value people put on a Black human life in 1735?

The *Southwell Frigate*

SOURCE 2

The *Southwell Frigate* was painted in 1760 by Nicholas Pocock, a West Indies sea captain. Up to 1749 the ship was a slave ship, and we know that in 1749 she transported 248 Africans from Calabar to Virginia (half of whom died on the Middle Passage). This is, therefore, a picture painted by someone who knew what he was talking about. It is interesting for the attitudes it shows to slavery and the Africans.

Activities

1. Study Source 2.
   a) Who do you think is the Black African second from right with the hat? What makes you think this?
   b) What is his relationship with the slave ship captain (third from right)? What makes you think this?
2. Compare the representation of the slave trade by the captain of a slave ship in Source 2 above with the painting by the Abolitionist George Morland on page 18.
   a) How do they show the scene differently?
   b) Why do they show the scene differently?
3. The African rulers were selling slaves. Does this mean they were to *blame* for the slave trade?

Enquiry: The Middle Passage

In *Roots*, some of the most horrific scenes are those which show the Middle Passage, including the terrible conditions below deck, the cruelty of the White sailors and the despair of the slaves.

How true is this picture of the Middle Passage? In Source 1, Olaudah Equiano continues his story of how he was carried into slavery.

Activity

If Equiano was not captured as a slave in Africa, and if he did not actually undergo the experiences he describes in Source 1, does that make Source 1 an unreliable source?

SOURCE 1

I was carried on board. I now thought that I had gotten into a world of bad spirits, and that they were going to kill me ... When I looked round the ship too and saw a large pot boiling, and many Black people chained together, every one of their faces showing dejection and sorrow, I no longer doubted of my fate ... I asked if we were going to be eaten by those White men with horrible looks, red faces, and loose hair ...

I now wished for the last friend, death, to save me; but soon, to my grief, two of the White men offered me eatables; and on my refusing to eat, one of them held me fast by the hands, and tied my feet, while the other flogged me severely ...

At last, when the ship we were in had got in all her cargo, we were all put under deck ... The lack of space, and the heat of the climate, added to the number in the ship, which was so crowded that each had scarcely room to turn himself, almost suffocated us. This produced great perspirations, so that the air soon became unfit for breathing, from a variety of loathsome smells, and brought on a sickness among the slaves, of which many died, thus falling victims to the foolish greed of their purchasers. This wretched situation was made worse by the rubbing of the chains, now become unbearable; and the filth of the necessary tubs, into which the children often fell, and were almost drowned. The shrieks of the women, and the groans of the dying, made the whole a scene of horror almost unthinkable ...

One day, two of my wearied countrymen who were chained together (I was near them at the time), jumped into the sea: immediately another quite dejected fellow, who, on account of his illness, was allowed to be out of irons, also followed their example ... Two of the wretches were drowned, but they got the other, and afterwards flogged him unmercifully for thus preferring death to slavery. In this manner we continued to undergo more hardships than I can now tell, hardships which are inseparable from this accursed trade.

Olaudah Equiano, *An Interesting Narrative* (1789).

Equiano was a Black African and former slave living in England, who wrote his book as part of the campaign to abolish the slave trade. There is evidence he was not transported from Africa, but was born a slave in America. However, he worked for many years as a sailor, and would have known about conditions on board a slave ship.

SOURCE 2

These plans of the slave ship *Brookes* packed with 454 slaves were prepared in 1789 by Thomas Clarkson, one of the leaders of the Abolitionists, for a report to Parliament. The pictures were printed onto 7,000 posters of the ship and published all over Britain.

The *Brookes* actually carried 740 slaves on one voyage. This had been done by locking them 'spoonwise' (that is sitting in lines between each other's knees). Another common way to 'tight pack' slaves was by making them lie on their sides, not on their backs.

After the Regulation Act of 1788, the *Brookes* was allowed to carry 454 slaves, which gave a space of 6 ft by 1 ft 4 inches (1.82 m by 0.40 m) to each man; 5 ft 10 inches by 1 ft 4 inches (1.77 m x 0.40 m) to each woman; and 5 ft by 1 ft 2 inches (1.52 m x 0.35 m) to each boy.

The *Brookes* was 100 ft (30 m) long (at points A–A) and 25 ft (8 m) wide (at points E–E), giving it deck space of about 3,000 square ft (280 m^2).

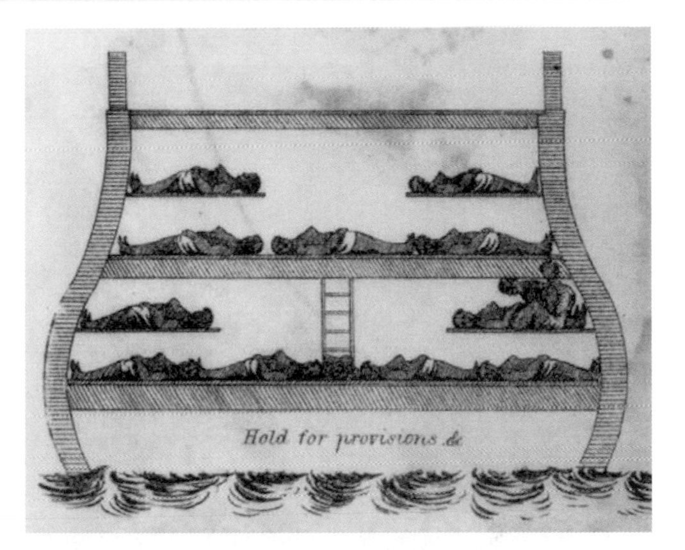

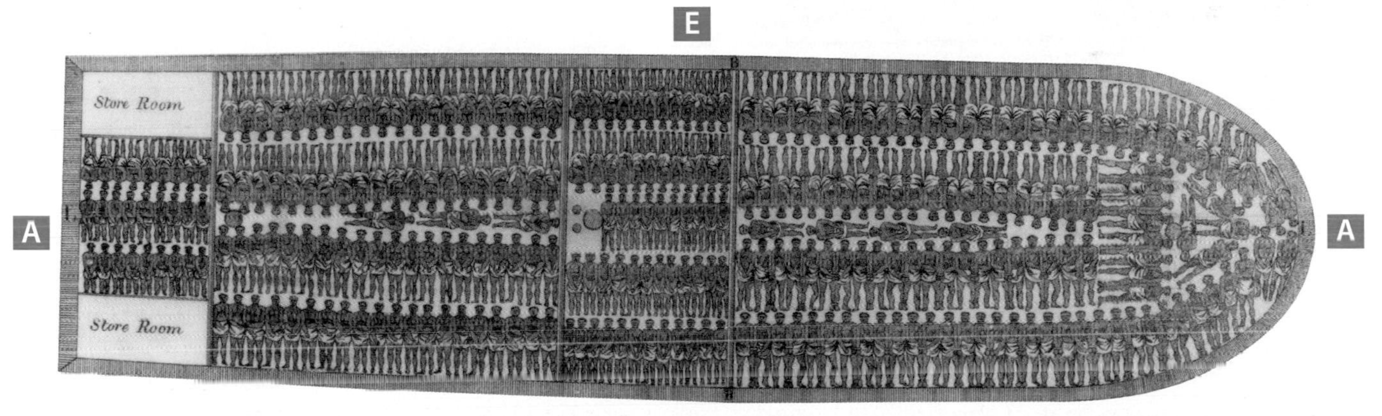

SOURCE 3

A drawing from about 1830 of slaves being loaded below deck. This was unlikely to have been based on eye-witness evidence.

SOURCE 4

'Scene in the hold of the blood-stained *Gloria*' – an artist's reconstruction of the scene in the hold of a slave-ship (the one described in Source 8 on page 25 by Richard Drake, who claimed to have sailed on it). It is likely that Drake's story was made up by an abolitionist, and that the unnamed artist had never been on a slave ship, but had imagined his picture from Drake's account.

SOURCE 5

We spent in our passage from … two months eleven days … in which time there happened much sickness and death among my poor men and Negroes, that of the first we buried 14, and of the last 320 … whereby the loss in all amounted to £6,560.

Captain Thomas Phillips, *A Voyage Made in the* Hannibal *1693–94* (1732).

Captain Phillips was a slave-trader.

SOURCE 6

To our great amazement above 100 men slaves jumped overboard … we lost 3 good men slaves, who would not try to save themselves, but resolved to die and sunk directly down.

Captain Japhet Bird, *Boston Weekly News Letter* (April 1737).

SOURCE 7

Some wet and blowing weather having caused the port-holes to be shut, fluxes (diarrhoea) and fevers among the Negroes followed. I often went down among them, till at length their apartments became so excessively hot as to be only bearable for a very short time … The floor of their rooms was so covered in the blood and mucus which had come from them because of the flux that it was like a slaughter-house.

Alexander Falconbridge, *An Account of the Slave Trade* (1788).

Falconbridge was a ship's doctor who had served on a slave ship, but left because he could not bear it.

Richard Phillips from the Anti-Slavery Society interviewed him and wrote up his memories.

By contrast, Falconbridge's wife enjoyed the company of slave-traders, and claimed that the slaves in Jamaica were far happier than the Blacks in Africa. Falconbridge died of drink in 1792.

SOURCE 8

Nothing but drinking and rioting could be seen among the men. They stripped themselves, and danced with black wenches …

The stench [in the hold] was hideous. The sick and dying were chained together. I saw pregnant women give birth to babes, whilst chained to corpses, which our drunken overseers had not removed. The blacks were literally jammed between decks, as if in a coffin; and a coffin that dreadful hold became, to nearly one-half of our cargo, before we reached Brazil.

The quarrelling that took place among the savages became sickening. They tore and gnawed each other in fights for rum-rations. Such scenes as I witnessed on that voyage can neither be told nor imagined.

Richard Drake, *Revelations of a Slave Smuggler* (1860).

This book claimed to have been 'dictated' by Drake, but historians doubt whether it is true. The people he describes actually existed, but historians think Drake is a made-up character, and that his 'story' was invented by Abolitionists to create opposition to slavery.

SOURCE 9

Slaves were taken up on deck and whipped to make them exercise.

This drawing of a French slave ship is dated 1837, and illustrated an article on the slave trade in a book on French shipping. France abolished the slave trade in 1826, so it is unlikely that the drawing is based on eye-witness evidence.

SOURCE 10

On board many ships, the common sailors are allowed to have sex with such of the black women whose agreement they can get [and] the officers are allowed to indulge their passions among them at pleasure; and are sometimes guilty of such brutal excesses as disgrace human nature.

Alexander Falconbridge, *An Account of the Slave Trade* (1788).

SOURCE 11

The case of the *Zong* has become one of the most infamous incidents of the Middle Passage. In 1781, the captain of the *Zong* found that many of his cargo were dying, so he threw 133 of them overboard.

If a slave died of natural causes or suicide, they were a 'dead loss' to their owners, but if a slave was killed by violence (e.g. to save the lives of the rest of the ship), then the owner could claim on the insurance.

When the *Zong's* insurers found out the trick, they refused to pay. The case ended up in court, where it came to the notice of Olaudah Equiano and the Abolitionists, who used it as evidence of the cruelty of the Middle Passage.

Activities

1. From Source 2 on page 23, using the tables and floor, persuade the class to lie down to recreate the way the slaves were packed onto the *Brookes* (for a journey of more than a month). How do you think the slaves would have felt?
2. Use the information in Sources 3–11 on pages 23–6 to create a dramatisation – in the form, for example, of a play or a diary – of a single slave's experience of the Middle Passage.
3. How do these accounts of the Middle Passage compare to Alex Haley's description on pages 6–7?
4. All the sources in this section were produced by Abolitionists, who often exaggerated conditions on the Middle Passage. Looking at the provenances of the sources on pages 23–6, give each source a 'reliability score' out of 5 (where '5' is 100 per cent reliable and 'zero' is a total lie). Explain your decisions.
5. The *Zong* case (Source 11) created a scandal. Does this suggest that it happened on every journey / on most journeys / on some journeys / rarely / just the once?

Interpretations: The Middle Passage revisited

How true is the accepted view of the Middle Passage?

The Case of John Kimber

SOURCE 1

This drawing is by the Abolitionist cartoonist Isaac Cruickshank, who had of course not witnessed the incident.

Kimber was captain of the slave ship *Recovery*, and took 300 slaves from Africa to the West Indies in 1791. During the voyage he whipped a female slave who was refusing to eat. In April 1792, a Bristol newspaper claimed that Kimber had hung her by the ankle and whipped her to death.

Kimber denied the accusation. In June 1792, Kimber's accuser – Thomas Dowling, the ship's surgeon – was found guilty of lying by the Court of the Admiralty. It was proved that he had told three people that 'he would be revenged upon Captain Kimber, and work his ruin'.

The court found that Dowling bore Kimber a grudge because the captain had only given him one female slave to have sex with, not two as he wanted. Kimber was found not guilty.

Activities

1. **Study Source 1. Describe how Cruickshank makes the scene look especially cruel and evil.**
2. **The court found Kimber 'not guilty'. Does this prove that he wasn't guilty of any crime?**
3. **Does this case prove that the Abolitionists 'exaggerated and lied'?**

Putting it in context

We should also consider the evidence that slave-traders needed to keep their slaves healthy to achieve a good price; and that sea conditions were terrible then for everyone – such as emigrants sailing to America, and the White sailors as well.

SOURCE 2

– That the Slave Ships at Liverpool are built on Purpose for this Trade, and are accommodated with Air Ports and Gratings for the Purpose of keeping the slaves cool …

– That the Slaves are comfortably lodged in Rooms fitted up for them, which are washed and fumigated every Day

– The Whole of the Slaves are brought upon Deck every Day, when Weather permits

– The Surgeon also generally attends to wash their Mouths with Vinegar or Lime Juice, in order to prevent Scurvy

– A warm meal is provided for them

– They are amused with instruments of Music of their own Country; and when tired of Music and Dancing, they then go to Games of Chance

– The Women are supplied with Beads, which they make into Ornaments; and the utmost Attention is paid to keeping up their Spirits

– That the Surgeon is provided with Medicines and with Wine and Spices also, for Cordials; and he is encouraged to take Care of the Sick, by an Allowance of One Shilling for every Slave that is brought to Market

– That the Reputation of the Captain, the Officers, the Surgeons, and their future Employment, depend on the Care they take of the Slaves

– That the Captain's Profit depends on the Value of the Cargo that is sold

– That it is so much to the Interest of the Captain and Officers to take Care of their Slaves that he does not think that any Law would enforce a kinder Treatment.

Evidence of James Penny, to the 1789 Parliamentary Committee.

Penny was a slave captain, who sailed two ships – the *Wilbrahim* and the *Nicholson* – on a number of voyages.

SOURCE 3

Evidence of James Penny to the 1789 Parliamentary Committee. These figures refer to his voyages in the *Wilbrahim* and *Nicholson* (1775–8), and the *Carolina* and *Pocketa* (1781–6).

	Slaves	Died	%age	Seamen	Died	%age
1775–76	531	27	5.1	40	7	17.5
1776–77	539	24	4.4	38	4	10.5
1777–78	560	31	5.5	48	3	6.3
1781–82	571	26	4.6	45	1	2.2
1785	209	1	0.5	20	3	15.0
1786	166	1	0.6	20	2	10.0

SOURCE 4

I've had the misforturn of burying seventy slaves; I am somewhat dissatisfied that it should happen to a young beginner but thank God it can't be said its owing to Neglect for sir I Can asure you that it has been the Constant Care and endevor for me for your Interest.

Captain Japhet Bird, letter to his employer, 27 February 1722.

SOURCE 5

Treat the Negroes with as much care as safety will allow and let none of your men abuse them under any excuse whatsoever. Be sure you see their food well made and given them in due season … make fires frequently in their rooms …

Instructions from the owners of the ship *Africa* to the captain, George Merrick (1774).

SOURCE 6

On board a slave ship – a nineteenth-century drawing by a little-known French artist, Pretexat Oursel. At least these slaves are being allowed on deck, but note the atrocity with the brick-bat.

SOURCE 7

... during the voyage there is on board these ships terrible misery, stench, fumes, horror, vomiting, many kinds of seasickness, fever, dysentery, headache, heat, constipation, boils, scurvy, cancer, mouth rot, and the like, so that many die miserably ... and many a time parents are compelled to see their children miserably suffer and die, and then to see them cast into the water.

Gottlieb Mittelberger, from his *Diary* (1754).

Gottlieb was a German organ teacher, describing the ships on which people emigrated to America. Every ship in those days was subject to over-crowding, and lack of sanitation and passengers often died of disease.

Activities

1. Discuss as a whole class whether you believe Captain Penny's evidence (see Sources 2 and 3) was likely to be accurate.
2. Discuss with a friend what Sources 4 and 5 tell you about the slave captains' incentives to look after their cargo.
3. How might you use Sources 3 and 7 to argue that sea travel was terrible for everyone in those days?
4. Imagine that you are the researcher for an MP who is due to attend a debate on the slave trade, and who wants to argue that the slave trade was not as bad as the Abolitionists were claiming. Use the evidence on these two pages to prepare a briefing paper for him.

Using evidence: Sold!

In *Roots*, Kunta Kinte's sale is treated as quite an amusing episode, when Kunta gets free and his captors are unable to catch him. But what was a slave sale *really* like?

SOURCE 1

Engraving of a 'scramble' (a sale of slaves) in the West Indies, *c.* 1810, showing slaves being inspected and families split.

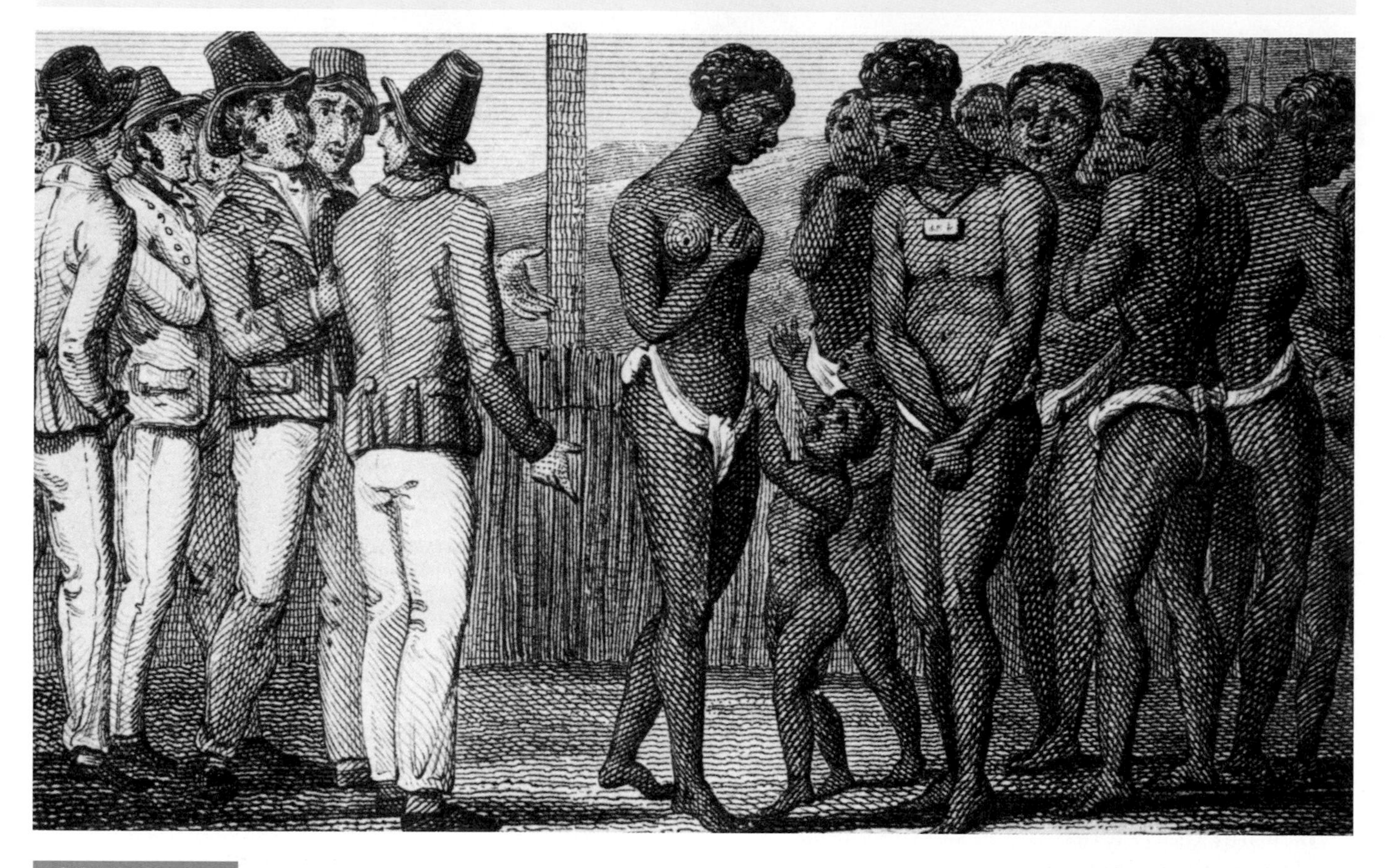

SOURCE 2

Tuesday, September 13th, 1774: Went ashore and saw a Cargo of Slaves land. One of the most shocking sights I ever saw. About 400 Men, Women and Children, brought from their native Country, deprived of their freedom, and themselves and their children become the property of cruel strangers without a chance of ever enjoying the Blessings of Freedom again, or a right of complaining, be their sufferings never so great … They were all naked, except for a piece of cloth about a foot broad to cover their nakedness, and appear much dejected.

Nicholas Cresswell, *Journal* (1774–77).

Cresswell was the son of a sheep farmer who went to America for the adventure. He was not an active Abolitionist, but he was a gentle and kind Methodist, and he thought the slave trade was 'cruel … shocking … a disgrace'.

Activity

Alex Haley's story of *Roots* may well have influenced the way we imagine the slave trade. Having studied the slave trade in great detail (pages 8–30), how reliable would you say *Roots* is as an interpretation of what the slave trade was like?

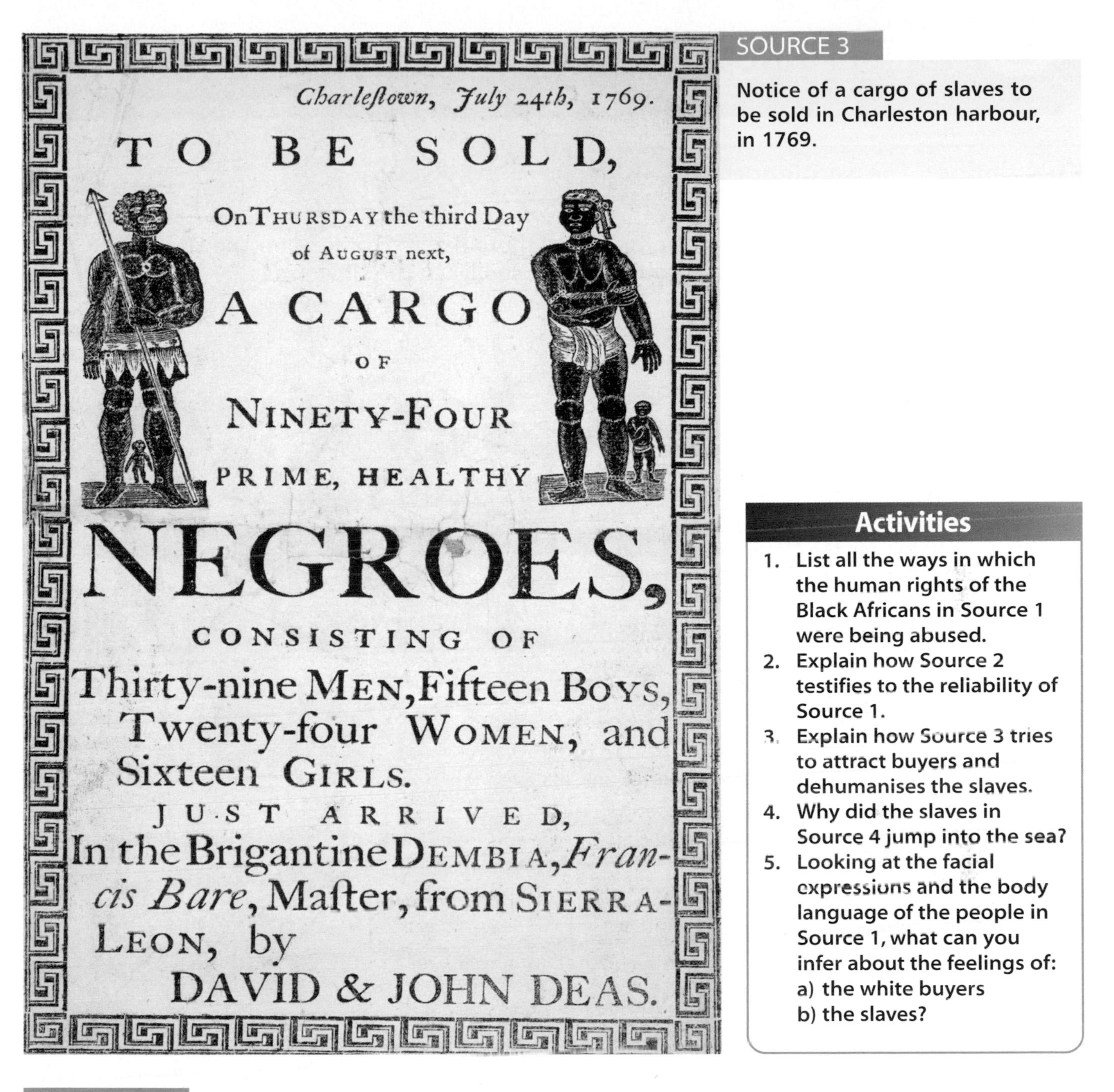

Charleſtown, July 24th, 1769.

TO BE SOLD,

On THURSDAY the third Day of AUGUST next,

A CARGO OF NINETY-FOUR PRIME, HEALTHY

NEGROES,

CONSISTING OF

Thirty-nine MEN, Fifteen BOYS, Twenty-four WOMEN, and Sixteen GIRLS.

JUST ARRIVED,

In the Brigantine DEMBIA, *Francis Bare*, Maſter, from SIERRA-LEON, by

DAVID & JOHN DEAS.

SOURCE 3

Notice of a cargo of slaves to be sold in Charleston harbour, in 1769.

Activities

1. List all the ways in which the human rights of the Black Africans in Source 1 were being abused.
2. Explain how Source 2 testifies to the reliability of Source 1.
3. Explain how Source 3 tries to attract buyers and dehumanises the slaves.
4. Why did the slaves in Source 4 jump into the sea?
5. Looking at the facial expressions and the body language of the people in Source 1, what can you infer about the feelings of:
   a) the white buyers
   b) the slaves?

SOURCE 4

As soon as the hour agreed on arrived, the doors of the yard were suddenly thrown open, and in rushed a large number of buyers, with all the fierceness of beasts … Some instantly seized such Negroes as they could conveniently lay hold of with their hands. Others, being prepared with several handkerchiefs tied together, encircled with these as many as they were able … The Negroes appeared extremely terrified, and near thirty of them jumped into the sea. But they were all soon retaken.

Alexander Falconbridge, *An Account of the Slave Trade* (1788).
Falconbridge was a ship's doctor who had served on a slave ship, but left because he could not bear it. Richard Phillips from the Anti-Slavery Society interviewed him and wrote up his memories.

Abolishing the slave trade

Knowledge: The sequence of Abolition

As you are thinking about whether the British ought to pay reparations for the slave trade, it is essential that you learn about how the British abolished the slave trade.

1772 The lawyer Granville Sharp argued that slavery was against English Law. The Courts said that a slave who escaped in England could not be forced to return to the West Indies, but they continued to allow slavery.

1774 John Wesley, the Methodist preacher, said that slavery was un-Christian.

1783 The *Zong* trial (see page 26) caused public outrage.

The Quakers (a religious group) presented a petition to Parliament (it was rejected).

1786 Thomas Clarkson decided to devote his life to ending the slave trade.

1787 *The Society for the Abolition of the Slave Trade* was founded. Granville Sharp was president. Clarkson and nine Quakers were on the Society's Committee.

William Pitt (the Prime Minister) asked William Wilberforce to lead the campaign in Parliament.

Josiah Wedgwood designed the seal: 'Am I not a man and a brother?'

Clarkson toured Britain, giving anti-slavery lectures and collecting information.

The 'Sons of Africa' – twelve Black Africans living in London – organised a letter-writing campaign against the slave trade.

1788 The Dolben Act limited the number of slaves a ship could carry.

The first Petition (60,000 signatures). The Committee organised public debates.

Hannah More wrote *Slavery – A Poem.* Many women supported abolition.

Parliament set up a Committee to look into the facts of the slave trade.

1789 Olaudah Equiano wrote *An Interesting Narrative*, which became a best-seller. He did a speaking tour of Britain.

The *Brookes* poster (see page 23) was published all over Britain.

George Morland painted *Execrable Human Traffic* (see page 18). Many artists and poets supported Abolition.

Wilberforce made a three-hour speech for Abolition in Parliament, but was defeated.

The French Revolution: opposed slavery, but it harmed the movement because it frightened people.

1791 The Parliamentary Committee finished its investigation – 1,000 pages of evidence. Clarkson summarised and published the key facts; his book became a best-seller.

The Haitian Revolution, led by the Black hero Toussaint L'Ouverture. This harmed the movement – people were worried at the sight of rebelling slaves.

Sugar boycott: 300,000 people joined the boycott.

1792 The 'Second Petition': 519 petitions were made to Parliament against the slave trade, signed by 390,000 people. Just four petitions supported the slave trade.

An Abolition Bill passed in the Commons, but it was defeated in the Lords.

1793 War with France. Clarkson retired. Wilberforce became ill. The campaign faded away for a while, although Wilberforce proposed Abolition Bills each year in the House of Commons.

1800 The price of a slave in Africa had risen to £25, but the sale price in America was stuck at around £35 – the slave trade was no longer very profitable.

1806 James Stephens suggested a different approach – a Bill to ban British subjects from trading with the French. Wilberforce persuaded Parliament to pass it. It stopped two-thirds of the slave trade.

1807 (25 March) The British Parliament banned the slave trade.

1808 The British West Africa Squadron was established to stop illegal slave trading. By 1865, it had freed 150,000 slaves.

1815 At the Congress of Vienna, Britain persuaded Spain, Portugal and France to agree to abolish the slave trade.

Activities

1. Make a list of PEOPLE involved in the Abolition movement, and what they did.
2. Make a list of TACTICS the Abolitionists used to try to get the slave trade abolished.
3. Some events actually harmed the movement – what were they?
4. Select the most important events, and design your own 'Timeline of Abolition'.

Causation: Why did the Abolition campaign succeed?

The Abolition campaign was the first public campaign in history, and it marked the start of many of our modern methods of campaigning.

1 The sugar boycott undermined the slave trade by damaging its profitability. The boycott particularly appealed to women, and was an early example of female public opinion 'flexing its muscles'.

2 The campaigners used plays, paintings and cartoons to get their message across. This made Abolition seem very cultured and fashionable.

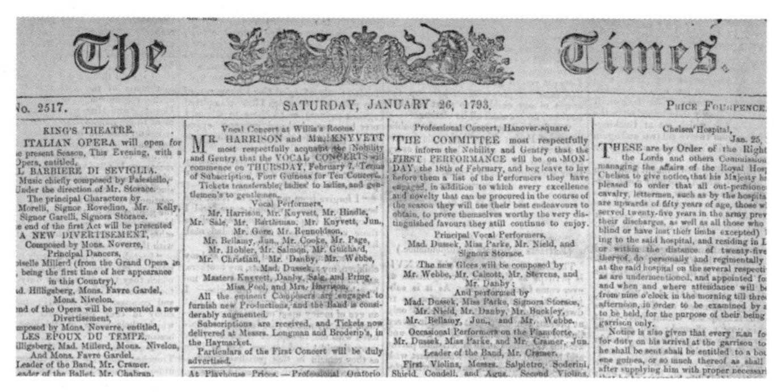

The Times.

No. 2517. SATURDAY, JANUARY 26, 1793. PRICE FOURPENCE.

KING'S THEATRE.
ITALIAN OPERA will open for
e present Season, This Evening, with a
Opera, entitled,
L BARBIERE DI SEVIGLIA.
Music chiefly composed by Paisiello,
Under the direction of Mr. Storace.
The principal Characters by
Morelli, Signor Rovedino, Mr. Kelly,
Signor Garelli, Signora Storace.
e end of the first Act will be presented
A NEW DIVERTISEMENT,
Composed by Mons. Noverre,
Principal Dancers,
iselle Millerd (from the Grand Opera in
, being the first time of her appearance
in this Country),
d. Hilligsberg, Mons. Favre Gardel,
Mons. Nivelon.
nd of the Opera will be presented a new
Divertisement,
mposed by Mons. Noverre, entitled,
LES EPOUX DU TEMPE.
illigsberg, Mad. Millerd, Mons. Nivelon,
And Mons. Favre Gardel.
Leader of the Band, Mr. Cramer.
eader of the Ballet, Mr. Chabran.

Vocal Concert at Willis's Rooms.
MR. HARRISON and Mr. KNYVETT most respectfully acquaint the Nobility and Gentry that the VOCAL CONCERTS will commence on THURSDAY, February 7. Terms of Subscription, Four Guineas for Ten Concerts. Tickets transferable; ladies' to ladies, and gentlemen's to gentlemen.
Vocal Performers,
Mr. Harrison, Mr. Knyvett, Mr. Hindle,
Mr. Sale, Mr. Bartleman, Mr. Knyvett, Jun.,
Mr. Gore, Mr. Rennoldson,
Mr. Bellamy, Jun., Mr. Cooke, Mr. Page,
Mr. Hobler, Mr. Salmon, Mr. Guichard,
Mr. Christian, Mr. Danby, Mr. Webbe,
Mad. Dussek,
Masters Knyvett, Danby, Sale, and Pring,
Miss Pool, and Mrs. Harrison.
All the eminent Composers are engaged to furnish new Productions, and the Band is considerably augmented.
Subscriptions are received, and Tickets now delivered at Messrs. Longman and Broderip's, in the Haymarket.
Particulars of the First Concert will be duly advertised.
At Playhouse Prices.—Professional Oratorio

Professional Concert, Hanover-square.
THE COMMITTEE most respectfully inform the Nobility and Gentry that the FIRST PERFORMANCE will be on MONDAY, the 18th of February, and beg leave to lay before them a list of the Performers they have engaged, in addition to which every excellence and novelty that can be procured in the course of the season they will use their best endeavours to obtain, to prove themselves worthy the very distinguished favours they still continue to enjoy.
Principal Vocal Performers,
Mad. Dussek, Miss Parke, Mr. Nield, and
Signora Storace.
The new Glees will be composed by
Mr. Webbe, Mr. Calcott, Mr. Stevens, and
Mr. Danby;
And performed by
Mad. Dussek, Miss Parke, Signora Storace,
Mr. Nield, Mr. Danby, Mr. Buckley,
Mr. Bellamy, Jun., and Mr. Webbe.
Occasional Performers on the Pianoforte,
Mr. Dussek, Miss Parke, and Mr. Cramer, Jun.
Leader of the Band, Mr. Cramer.
First Violins, Messrs. Salpietro, Soderini,
Shield, Condell, and Agus. Second Violins,

Chelsea Hospital,
Jan. 25,
THESE are by Order of the Right
the Lords and others Commission
managing the affairs of the Royal Hos
Chelsea to give notice, that his Majesty h
pleased to order that all out-pensione
cavalry, lettermen, such as by the hospita
are upwards of fifty years of age, those w
served twenty-five years in the army prev
their discharges, as well as all those who
blind or have lost their limbs excepted)
ing to the said hospital, and residing in L
or within the distance of twenty-five
thereof, do personally and regimentally
at the said hospital on the several respecti
as are undermentioned, and appointed fo
and when and where attendance will b
from nine o'clock in the morning till thre
afternoon, in order to be examined by
to be held, for the purpose of their being
garrison only.
Notice is also given that every man fo
for duty on his arrival at the garrison to
he shall be sent shall be entitled to a bo
one guinea, or so much thereof as shall
after supplying him with proper necessari

3 More people were learning to read, and the campaigners knew how to get stories of atrocities into the newspapers. They also organised letter-writing campaigns.

4 The Committee to Abolish the Slave Trade led the campaign. It raised money, organised public events and lobbied Members of Parliament.

The Black Slave Trade
by Hannah More (1788)

Whenever to Africa's shore I turn my eyes
Horrors of deepest, deadliest guilt arise.
I see, by more than Imagination shown,
The burning village, and the blazing town;
See the poor victim torn from social life,
See the scared infant, see the shrieking wife!
She, poor wretch! is dragged by hostile hands
To distant tyrants sold in distant lands!

5 The campaign used poems and books to get the message across. This appealed to both men and women.

6 The idea of a petition to Parliament was not new, but the Abolitionists gathered hundreds of thousands of signatures – the first really public campaign.

7 **The Abolitionists were supported by lawyers like Granville Sharp, and used the courtroom and the law to fight their case.**

8 **The Abolitionists knew that, ultimately, nothing could happen unless Parliament passed a law to abolish the slave trade. They asked Wilberforce to lead the campaign in Parliament.**

9 **A Parliamentary Committee was set up to investigate the slave trade. The Abolitionists believed that *facts* would win their argument.**

10 **When he brought chains and irons to illustrate his speeches, Clarkson pioneered the use of visual aids, the most effective being the picture (and later, the model) of the *Brookes*.**

11 **The Committee's seal, with its emotive logo, became particularly powerful when Wedgwood had the brilliant idea of turning it into a cameo – a fashion accessory – which sold in tens of thousands.**

12 **Many of the supporters of Abolition were strong Christians, who felt slavery was un-Christian. Religion was an important influence on people in those times.**

Activities

1. For each of the 'methods of campaigning' explain HOW it might have helped the Abolitionists to win their argument. Which do you think was the most effective method?
2. Design your own 'campaigning idea' for Abolition and present it as eye-catchingly as possible – think of the cleverest idea you can.

Interpretations: Heroes of Abolition

Wilberforce or Wilberfest?

The year 2007 was the bi-centenary of the Abolition of the Slave Trade. It was a time of pride in Britain – the first country to abolish the slave trade.

The Wilberforce Society (which campaigns to end the slavery that still exists even today) produced lots of materials. Christian churches held services of apology and reconciliation.

But was too much attention paid to Wilberforce? Had the celebrations – meant to be a festival of Abolition – become a 'Wilberfest'?

Ioan Gruffudd, star of the comic-book film *The Fantastic Four*, played a dashing and emotional Wilberforce. Critics pointed out that in real life Wilberforce was aloof, a moral prig, and held opinions we would regard as racist today.

A film called *Amazing Grace* told the story of the Abolition of the Slave Trade. Wilberforce was made out to be the star of the show – the man to whom everybody turned for leadership; the man who formed and led the Committee to Abolish the Slave Trade; the man who guided the Act through Parliament.

Critics pointed out that Wilberforce only led the campaign *in Parliament*; that it was the Quakers and Clarkson who formed and ran the Committee; and that it was Stephens who got the Act through Parliament – Wilberforce was not very good as a Parliamentary strategist.

Historians suggested that much more attention ought to have been paid to the vitally important roles played by other people in the Abolition movement – notably by Black British people, and by women.

Heroes of their time

History is a matter of interpretation, and each age chooses its heroes to suit itself. Is this because, with hindsight, we can see things that people at the time did not see? Or is it because, by selecting heroes who appeal to us, we choose people we think *ought* to have been important, and maybe were not so important at the time?

Activities

1. What do you notice about the heroes in Source 1?
2. What do you notice about the heroes in Source 2?
3. What does the sources' choice of heroes tell us about how society has changed, 1875–2007?

SOURCE 1

Heroes of the Slave Trade Abolition.

This poster was produced in about 1875.

Zachary Macaulay had managed a sugar plantation but became a Christian, and rose to be Secretary of the Committee to abolish the Slave Trade.

Thomas Fowell Buxton was a friend of Wilberforce who married into an important Quaker family.

SOURCE 2

Abolition of the Slave Trade.

This set of stamps was issued to commemorate the bi-centenary of abolition in 2007. *Left to right*: William Wilberforce, Olaudah Equiano, Granville Sharp, Thomas Clarkson, Hannah More, Ignatius Sancho.

Ignatius Sancho was born on a slave ship *en route* to the West Indies. He bought his freedom, and became a grocer in England. After his death, his letters to other Abolitionists were published and had a great effect on public opinion. (You can find out about the other Abolitionists on pages 38–39.)

A roll-call of some heroes (in alphabetical order)

Thomas Clarkson

The moral powerhouse of the movement, fact-finder and publicist.

- Founding member of the Abolition Committee.
- Collected evidence and organised the petitions.
- Wrote many books and pamphlets.
- Designed the picture of the *Brookes*.

Olaudah Equiano

The best-selling author.

- A former slave who had worked as a sailor all over the world.
- Founder of the 'Sons of Africa' – Black British people who campaigned against the slave trade.
- Wrote *An Interesting Narrative*, and spoke all over Britain.

Toussaint L'Ouverture

The real revolutionary who first seized freedom for Black slaves.

- A slave who led a revolution in French Saint Domingue (1791) and set up the first free Black state in the Americas.
- His example inspired the French Revolution to free all France's slaves in 1794.

Hannah More

Influential poet who opposed the slave trade.

- A teacher who became a Christian.
- Inspired many women to oppose the slave trade.
- Helped organise the sugar boycott.
- Friend of both Wilberforce and Clarkson – stopped them falling out with each other.

Granville Sharp

One of the first Abolitionists – known as 'the father of the movement'.

- **Defended ex-slaves in the courts; established that a slave was free when he set foot on English soil.**
- **Took the captain of the *Zong* to court for murder.**
- **Helped set up a settlement of freed slaves in Sierra Leone.**
- **Founder-member and first chairman of the society for the Abolition of the Slave Trade.**

James Stephen

The political strategist who coached the cause through its end game.

- **A lawyer in the West Indies, who was horrified by the way the slaves were treated.**
- **Returned to England and became an MP and member of the Abolition Committee.**
- **Designed the final strategy in Parliament, which asked only to ban the trade with Britain's enemies.**

Josiah Wedgwood

A brilliant businessman who helped to 'sell' the cause.

- **Gave money to the Abolition Committee and became one of its members.**
- **Designed the famous 'Am I not a Man and a Brother?' seal.**
- **Made the design into cameos – made Abolition fashionable.**

William Wilberforce

MP for Hull, leader of the Parliamentary campaign.

- **A strong Christian.**
- **Also supported prison reform and the RSPCA; called 'the conscience of Parliament'.**
- **Friend of the Prime Minister William Pitt, who asked him to lead the campaign in Parliament.**
- **Presented the Abolition Committee's findings in the House of Commons.**
- **Presented a Bill to abolish the slave trade every year from 1788 to 1807.**

Activity

Debate as a whole class:
Who do you think was the most important hero of the Abolition of the Slave Trade?
Who was the 'Weakest Link'? Who had the abolition 'X-factor'? Choose your 'Abolitionist Hero for the twenty-first century'.

4 Four kinds of slavery

There has been slave labour in society from before Roman times right through to the present day, when there are still instances of 'sweatshop' labour. How did the eighteenth-century trade compare with other forms of slavery?

Roman slavery

The Romans (509BC–AD476) depended on slavery. There were perhaps 10 million slaves in the Roman Empire, and 40 per cent of the people of Rome were slaves.

The Romans took slaves from the races they conquered. Slaves were expensive: a good farm slave cost 2,000 denarii (worth about £2,000 today), although a good-looking and talented boy might cost twenty times as much.

Many slaves worked for the government as police and officials. Slaves did all the manual labour of the empire – they swept the streets, carried, farmed, built. But educated Greek slaves were employed as tutors and doctors; other slaves were employed as dancers and musicians. The Romans never let their slaves fight in the army – they did not want to put weapons into slaves' hands.

Slaves working in the mines and farms were treated badly – one writer told farmers to give their slaves a new tunic and shoes every other year. Household slaves were better treated. At the December festival of Saturnalia, masters waited on their slaves for a day.

Slaves had few rights. Until *c.* AD50, a Roman master was allowed to beat his slaves to death, and to throw them out to die when they became too old to work. If a slave killed his master, every slave in that household was put to death, and slave rebellions were punished by mass crucifixions.

Roman slaves could not marry, and any children born to them were slaves. Slaves could not own anything, but some masters gave them spending money, which they saved up and used to buy their freedom. Sometimes a master would give his slaves their freedom as a gift, or in his will.

Roman slaves building a wall.

Arab slavery

An engraving of Arab slave-traders from the nineteenth century.

The Arab slave trade lasted from the seventh to the twentieth century – Saudi Arabia only abolished slavery in the 1960s. In all, perhaps 14 million Black Africans were taken to the Middle East as slaves. Many boy slaves were castrated, so that they could work as eunuchs in the household harems (ladies' rooms) and in the mosques. Islamic law forbade a master to castrate a slave, so Arab slave-traders set up castration stations at the border, and the boys were castrated before they were sold; many died from the operation. At least 15 per cent of captured slaves died before they could be sold.

Slaves were expensive – in 1860, a strong African male cost $300 (about £3,800 today), while pretty white-skinned girls and eunuchs cost up to ten times as much.

Slaves were used as house servants, labourers and soldiers. The law allowed a master to use his female slaves for sex. Household slaves were often well-treated, and some even rose to be business partners of their masters. But slaves employed on farm plantations or in the mines were badly treated, and no slave employed in the salt mines of the Sahara Desert lived longer than five years.

Black slaves were held to be sub-human, though higher than an animal. A slave could not own anything, and the value of a slave if killed was only half that of a human being. On the other hand, Arabian slaves had (low) social status and (some) legal rights. Islamic law forbade a master to be cruel to a slave. Slaves had the right to medicine when sick and care when old.

Slaves could buy their freedom, or be given it by their master. If slaves were mistreated, the law theoretically gave them their freedom. The child of a slave was also a slave. However, many slave girls married their masters, and the law said that to do so he had first to grant her freedom, so their children would be born free.

African slavery

African slaves.

Slavery was common in Africa from the time of the Egyptians and still exists today. It has been estimated that, between 1500 and 1900, 8 million Africans were made slaves to other Africans. In the nineteenth century, in some places, slaves made up two-thirds of the population.

Many slaves were captured on slave raids on nearby tribes; it is thought that on average 15 per cent of the captured slaves died during their capture and sale. During famines, however, people would offer themselves as slaves to wealthy men.

Slaves were cheap, although the price rose to £25 in 1800 (about £1,200 today).

African slave-owners preferred women, because women did the farming and housework. Women slaves were used for sex. African kings built up large armies of royal slaves and used them to attack other tribes, so that they could capture people and sell them on as slaves to British and French slave-traders.

African slaves were not the 'possessions' of other people, and not for life. Their 'owner' was more like a feudal lord in medieval Europe, giving food and protection in return for labour; this helped improve the way they were treated.

Slaves were often protected by the customs of the tribe. Slaves in Ethiopia could go where and when they pleased, as long as they did not try to escape.

Many slaves bought their freedom, and lived as free men and women in the tribe – some even rose to become kings. It was quite common for a master to marry a slave, in which case his wife would stay a slave, but his children would be free.

Transatlantic slavery

The Transatlantic slave trade lasted from the sixteenth century until 1807. Perhaps 12 million Black Africans were taken to be slaves in the Americas.

On average 15 per cent of the captured Africans died on the sea voyage to America, but the numbers dying fell from one in four (25 per cent) in the seventeenth century to one in twenty (5 per cent) by the end of the eighteenth century.

When they reached the Americas, the slaves were sold at auction. They were expensive – in 1790, a strong male slave cost $215 (about £5,000 today).

Most slaves became field labourers. Some slaves were used as house servants. Many White masters used their female slaves for sex.

Field slaves were given two sets of clothes, for summer and winter, and a new blanket every third year. Household slaves were often better treated, but even small mistakes might result in terrible punishment – the law allowed a slave-owner to beat a slave to death. Slaves who tried to run away were lamed, mutilated or killed as an example.

Slaves could not own anything, and were listed along with the farm animals as their master's possessions. They were held to be little higher than apes – the American constitution considered a 'Negro' man three-fifths of a person. Few slaves were given their freedom; the child of a slave was also a slave, and none ever married their masters.

The Transatlantic slave trade.

Activities

All forms of slavery are a crime against humanity, but have some been nastier than others?

1. **The following is a list of factors on which you might make a judgement about how bad a particular form of slavery was:**
   - **duration**
   - **numbers**
   - **cruelty of the trade**
   - **prices**
   - **jobs**
   - **treatment**
   - **legal rights**
   - **chances of freedom.**

   List the factors above in order of importance when making this judgement.
2. **Make notes for all four forms of slavery in the form of a 4 x 8 grid using the eight factors in Question 1.**
3. **Compare the four forms of slavery. For each factor in each form of slavery, award a 'nastiness mark' out of 5 – from '5' (diabolical) to '0' (not nasty at all, really).**
4. **Debate which was the nastiest form of slavery of all time, taking into account that some factors are more important than others.**

5 The reckoning

Results of the slave trade

Africa

Social effects

The slave trade ruined African society:

1. The countryside was swept by wars, which led to frequent famines.
2. It destroyed tribal customs.
3. It kept African rulers weak, which made them easy prey for attackers.

Economic effects

The slave trade stopped the African economy having an Industrial Revolution as in Europe:

1. Africa only produced/sold people.
2. It took the young and the healthy, and left the weak and the old.
3. It provided metal and cloth, so Africa stopped producing these.
4. It reduced the population, which held back economic development.

Britain

Social effects

The slave trade financed British society:

1. It supplied Britain with sugar, tobacco and rum.
2. It paid for the social life of the rich slave-traders.
3. Rich slave-traders got involved in local government and became MPs.
4. Black people came to live in Britain.
5. It encouraged racism among White British people.

Economic effects

The slave trade helped to stimulate an Industrial Revolution in Britain:

1. It provided wages for ship-builders, sail-makers, rope-makers, dockers and thousands of sailors.
2. The rich slave ship owners spent their profits, which stimulated the British economy.
3. Industry was stimulated when slave-traders bought the metal and cloth to exchange for slaves in Africa.
4. Liverpool and Bristol grew into large wealthy towns.

Activities

'The rich slave ship owners spent their profits, which stimulated the British economy.'

1. List everything you can see in this Hogarth painting – it all had to be bought and paid for.
2. For each object, think which trades and industries would be stimulated by its purchase (e.g. buying the table would have helped a carpenter, but also the timber-grower).

A painting by Hogarth, 1733. The rich man's mistress kicks over a table to let her lover get away unnoticed. Notice the fashionable Black boy servant.

First thoughts: How much would compensation cost?

A United Nations World Conference Against Racism was held in South Africa in 2001. One of the key speeches was made by Zimbabwe's Minister of Justice.

> *'The slave trade [was] a crime against humanity. A legal obligation to pay reparations should be placed on those countries who engaged in these evil practices.'*
>
> **P A Chinamasa, Zimbabwe's Minister of Justice.**

But if Britain were to agree to pay compensation, how much might that involve?
Here are some recent examples of compensation sums awarded or claimed:

WRONGFUL ARREST

A pub landlord and his family got £47,000 compensation from Lancashire police for assault and false charges by police officers, when they were wrongfully arrested.

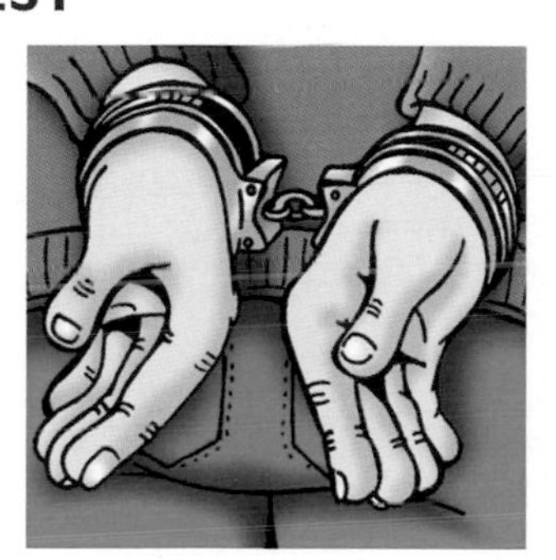

PHYSICAL INJURY

Mrs K from Southampton, who suffered a serious head injury in an accident at work (which gave her 'severe headaches'), was awarded compensation of £73,492.

KIDNAP

Austrian kidnap victim Natascha Kampusch, kidnapped aged 10 and imprisoned by her kidnapper for more than eight years, claimed £450,000 in compensation.

DEATH

When Iraqi civilians were killed in a shoot-out involving a US security contractor, an Iraqi report called for £4 million in compensation for each of the 17 Iraqis who died.

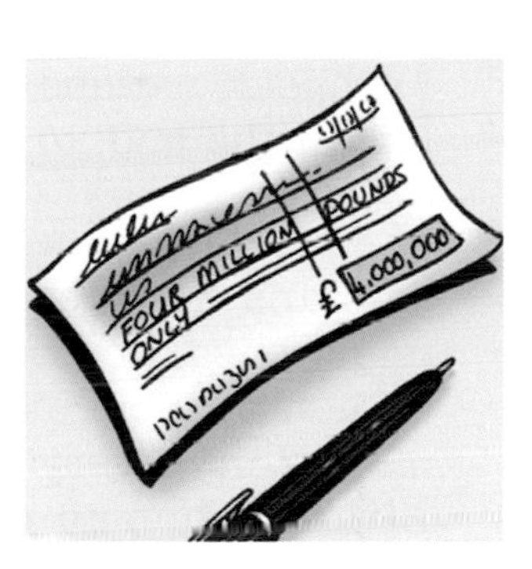

Activities – Using this book

1. Consider the personal experiences of an individual slave (see especially pages 18–31) to make a list of the different hurts/indignities for which each slave might claim compensation.
   For each hurt, allot a reasonable payment for compensation, and then total these to come up with a 'sum per person'. Multiply this sum by 3 million (the number of slaves transported on British ships).
2. In addition, perhaps a sixth of all slaves on the Middle Passage died. Allot a reasonable sum per death and multiply this sum by 500,000 deaths.
3. Look at the effects the slave trade had on Africa (see page 44). Estimate a reasonable overall sum for the damage done to Africa's economy and society.
   Add up the amounts in Questions 1, 2 and 3 to calculate a 'Total Reparations Payment'.

Debate: Should we consider paying reparations?

Arguments FOR the British paying reparations

1. The slave trade ruined Africa. It took away half the population. It took the youngest, strongest people, and left the old, the children and the sick. Africa never recovered, was left open to conquest in the next century and STILL bears the economic and social scars.

2. The slave trade ruined life even for those Africans who were not sold into slavery. In constant danger, many of them stopped bothering to work. Some sold their children into slavery for a bottle of brandy.

3. Slavery was wrong BY NATURE. There is no defence for it.

4. Slavery was racist. Only Black Africans were captured and sold.

5. The slave trade treated the Black slaves like animals, but it also brutalised the slave-traders, who became like animals in a different way.

6. The slave trade gave the British huge wealth, and helped cause the Industrial Revolution, while Africa became impoverished.

7. The slave trade put the African nations under the control of European nations. They suffered a crucial loss of power which led, in the end, to colonialism.

8. The slave trade was a crime against humanity. Twelve million Africans were torn from their homes and their families, imprisoned, abused, beaten and kept in inhuman conditions. Two million of them died on the voyage, and many more died later in misery in slavery. The slave trade was a mass-violation of the Africans' human rights.

Activities – Debate

1. **Divide into two groups, one 'for' and one 'against' Britain paying reparations for the slave trade to the Black population. Working with a friend, discuss the ideas on pages 46–7 which support 'your' case. Try to find, in this book, facts which prove the points.**
2. **Looking back through the book, think of some other points to make about whether Britain should pay reparations for the slave trade.**
3. **Coming together as a whole class, debate the idea: should Britain pay reparations for the slave trade – and if so, how much?**
4. **Does your opinion depend on what section of 'British' society you come from?**

Arguments AGAINST the British paying reparations

1. What was so good about Africa before the slave trade? It was less economically developed, swept by tribal wars and had some vicious rulers.
2. There is evidence that the slave-trade was only a small factor in Africa's economy at the time; other trades such as salt and the gum trade were also very important.
3. You cannot convict the slave-traders for a 'crime against humanity' when few people at the time thought slavery was wrong, or understood the concept of a 'crime against humanity'.
4. Slaves were not just traded by White Europeans. The African kings captured slaves from other African tribes and sold them to the White traders. One American writer says that Black Africans ought to apologise to Black Americans for the slave trade.
5. You cannot punish modern Europeans for something that happened hundreds of years ago, and that they would not have done themselves.
6. The British were not the only nation which was involved in the slave trade – the French, Danish, Portuguese, Spanish and Arabs also traded slaves. After 1807, the British spent the rest of the century trying to STOP the slave trade.
7. Stories of the cruelties and horror were exaggerated by the Abolitionists. No more people died on slave voyages than on other voyages at that time, and traders took care of their slaves.
8. The British did not steal the slaves – they *bought* them from the African rulers in what both sides regarded as a business deal, and pumped millions of pounds into the African economy of the time.

Activities – Summing it all up

1. **On pages 4–5, at the beginning of this course, you were asked to suggest a caption for this painting. Look back at what you wrote. At the end of the course, do you still feel that your caption is appropriate? Think of a new, better-informed caption.**
2. **On page 4 you were also asked to write down your 'first thoughts' about the slave trade. Look back at what you wrote. At the end of the course, do you still agree with what you wrote?**
3. **If you had to sum up your thoughts about the slave trade now, what would you say? Write down your new, better-informed ideas in less than 50 words.**

Understanding: How significant was the slave trade?

Significance involves five ideas. Something is historically significant if it is (or has) the following.

1. **Revealing (does it tell you a lot about history?)**
   How much have you learned about Britain and Africa by studying the slave trade? Scan back through the book and select the TWO most important facts that you have learned.

2. **Results (did it have a big effect?)**
   Search back through the book looking for consequences of the slave trade. Look especially at pages 16–17, 43 and 44. Choose TWO results which you feel were especially important.

3. **Remarkable (was it important at the time?)**
   Scan back through the book, looking first at the primary evidence from the time on pages 18–31. Look also at the information on pages 32–35 and 37. Choose TWO good examples of facts or sources which give the impression that people at the time thought that the events were important.

4. **Remembered (do people still remember it today?)**
   I suppose the fact that you are studying it now proves they do! But how remembered is the slave trade? Find TWO clues that it is – try looking on pages 4, 6–7, 36, 37, 45 or 48.

5. **Relevant (are the issues it raises still important for us today?)**
   Scan back through the book to remind yourself of those issues which the information about the slave trade raised in your mind. Share TWO of them with the class or a friend. How relevant are these issues to us, in our world, today?

Activities – How significant was the slave trade?

1. **How are the demonstrators in the picture above showing they are sorry for the slave trade?**
2. **Using the ideas and information in points 1–5 on this page, have a class discussion about how significant an historical event the slave trade was.**